WHY WE SWEAR?

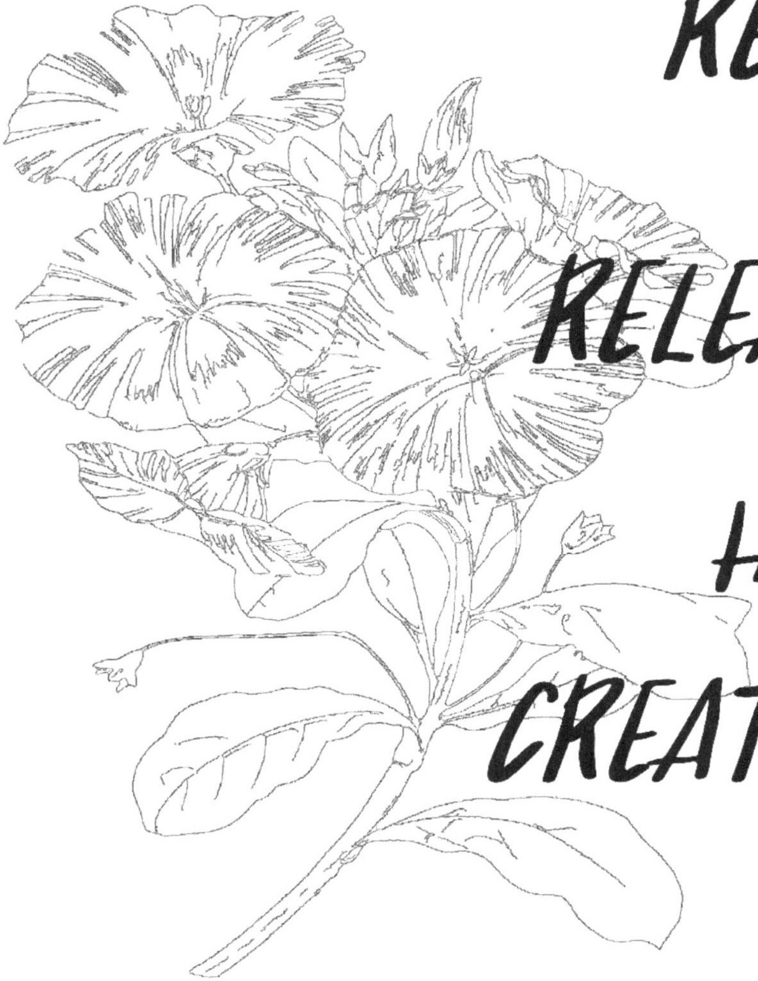

RELAX

RELEASE

HAVE FUN

CREATE

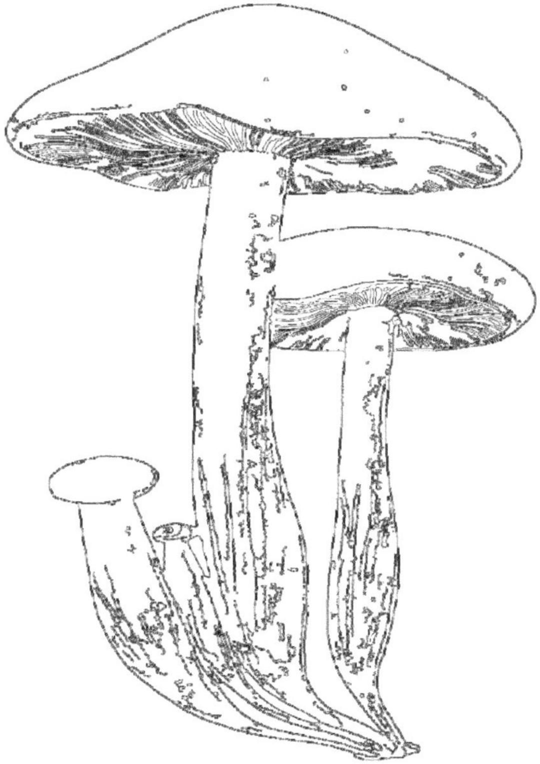

ENJOY COLORING !!!

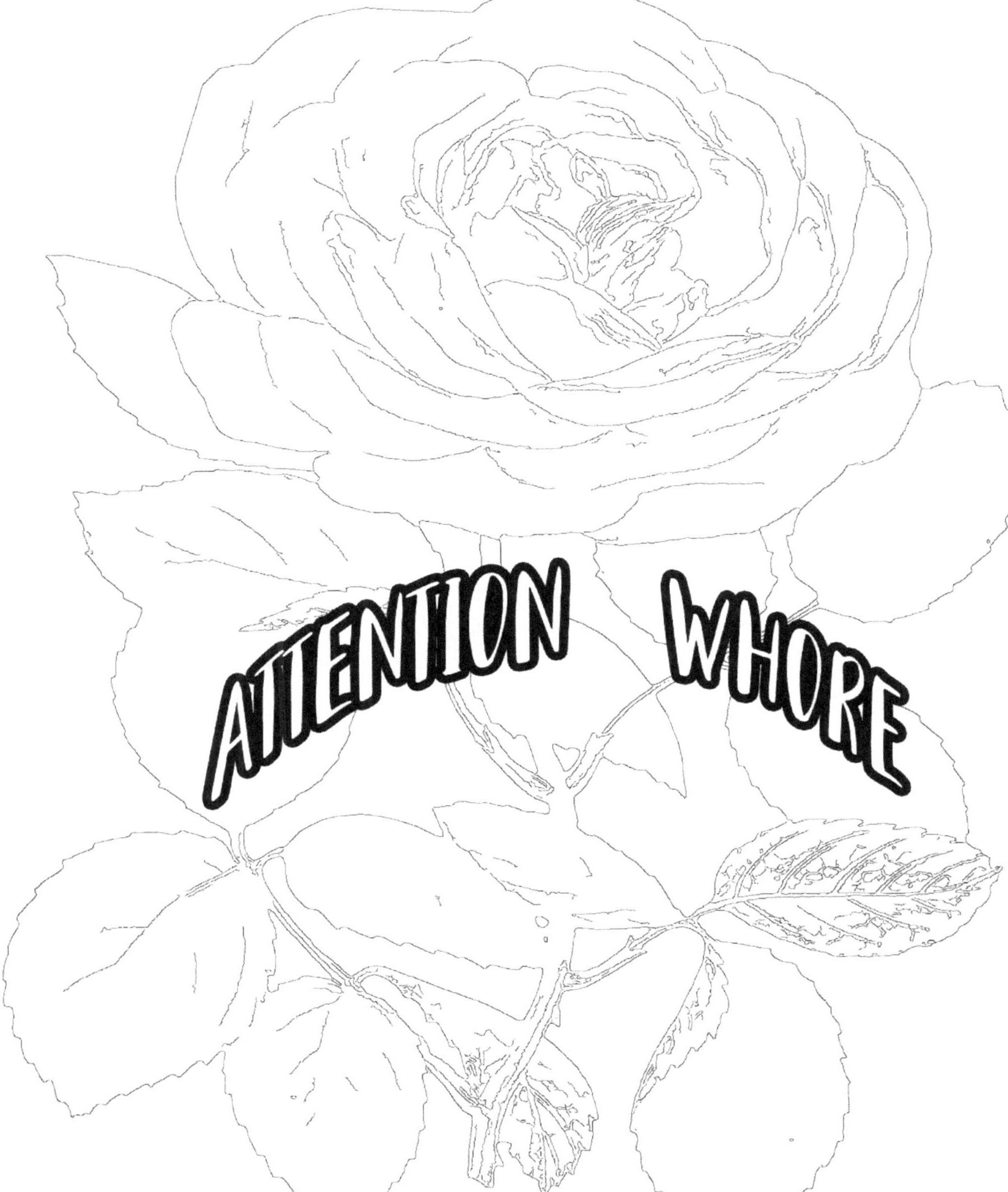
ATTENTION WHORE

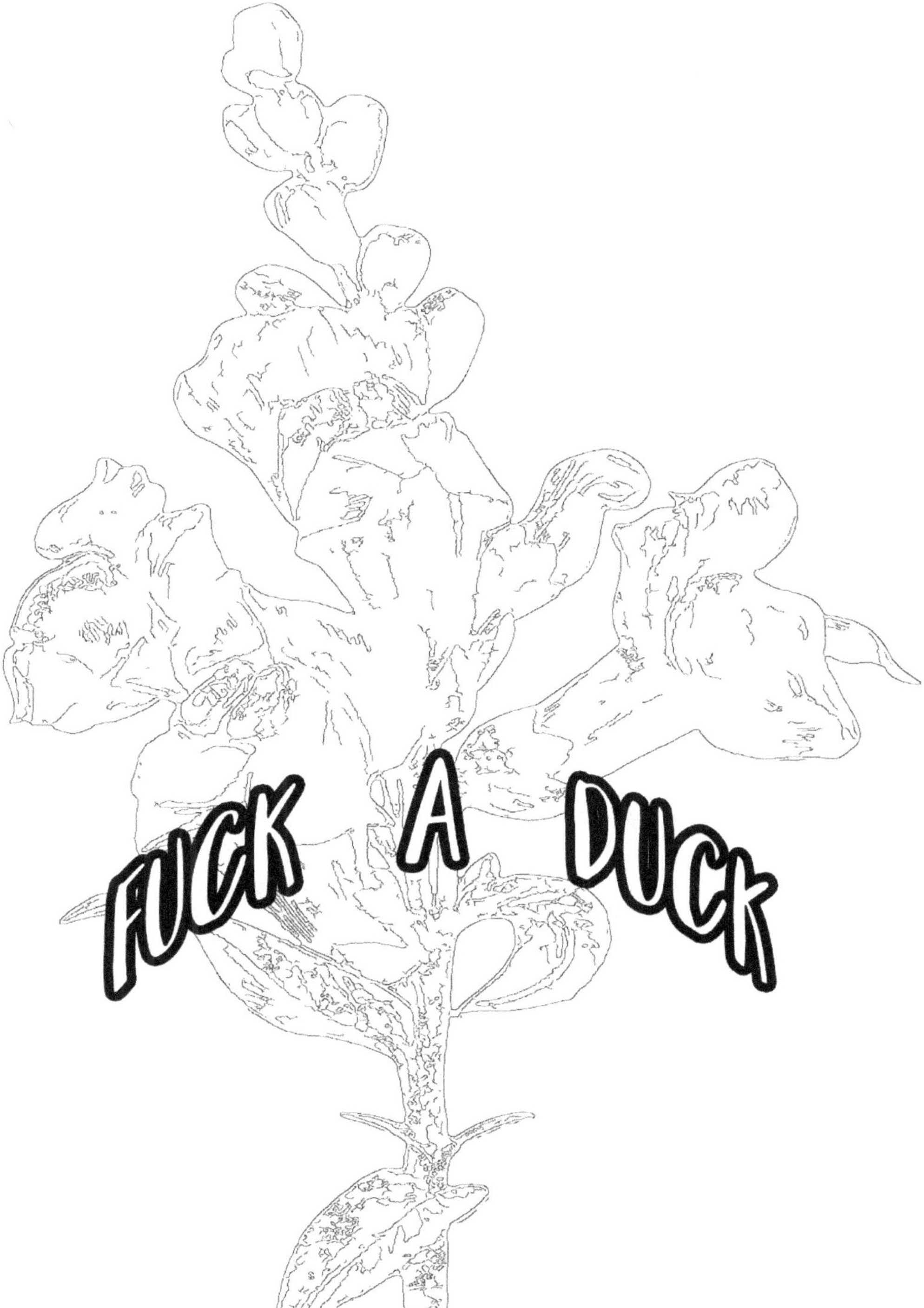
FUCK A DUCK

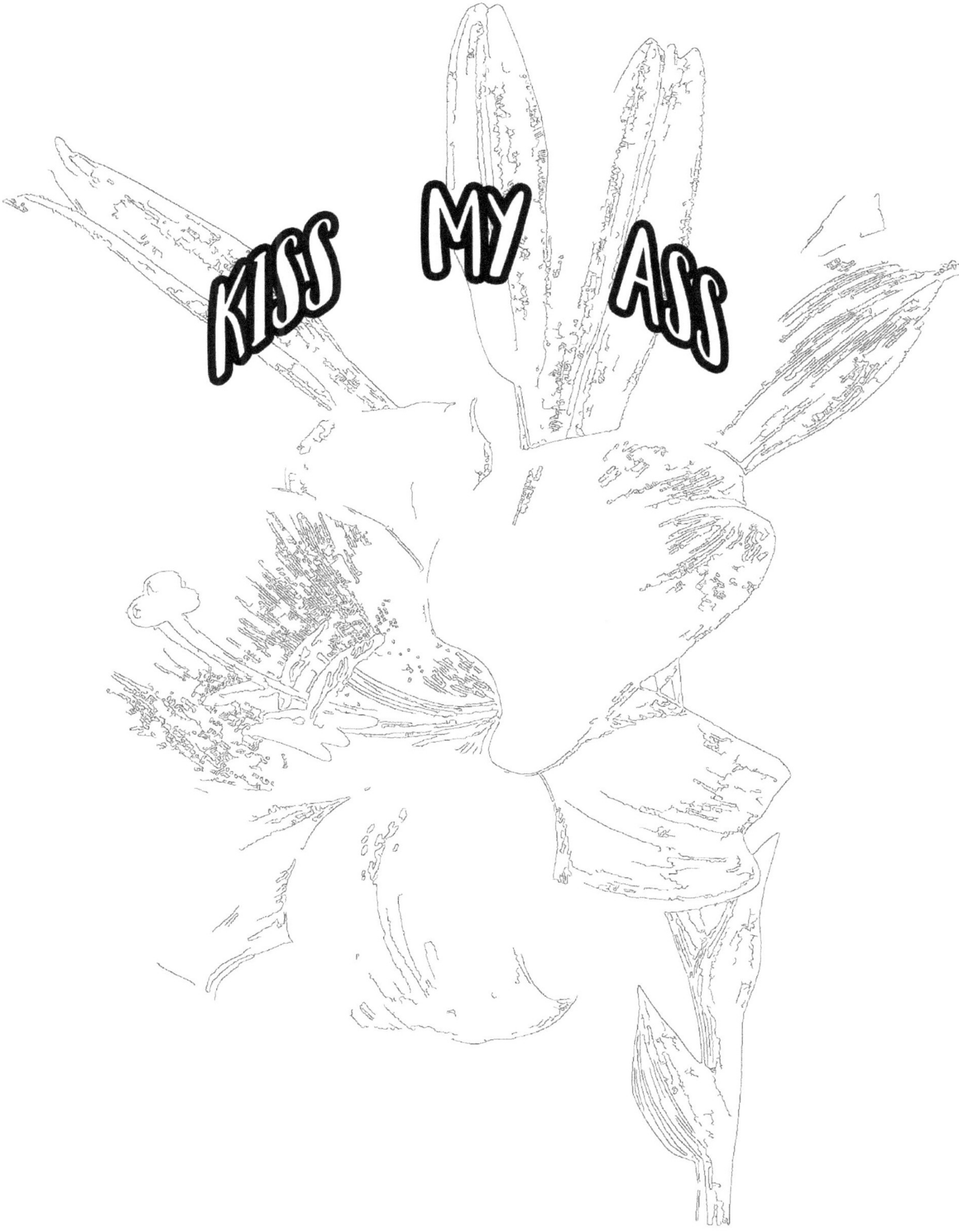
KISS MY ASS

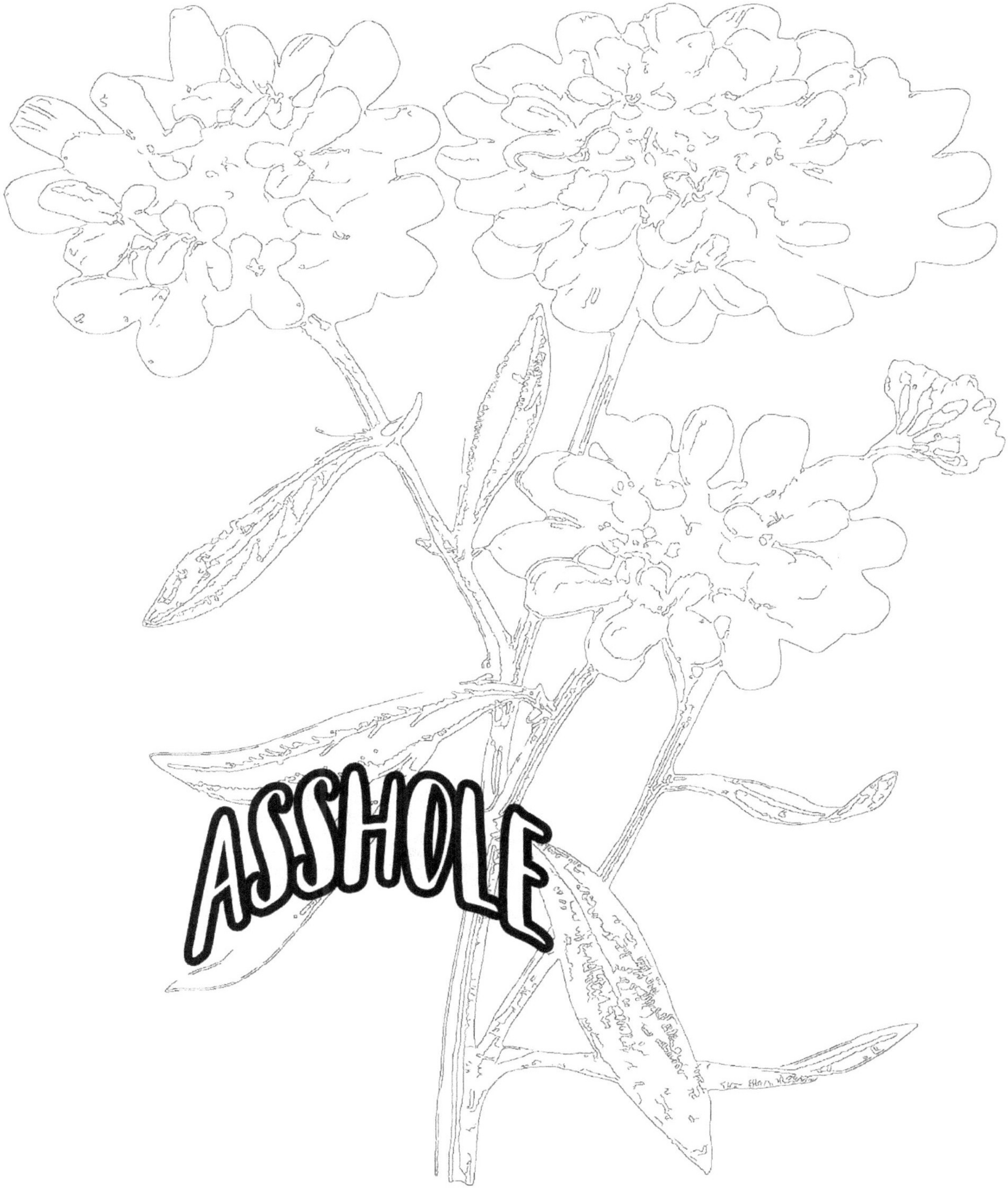
ASSHOLE

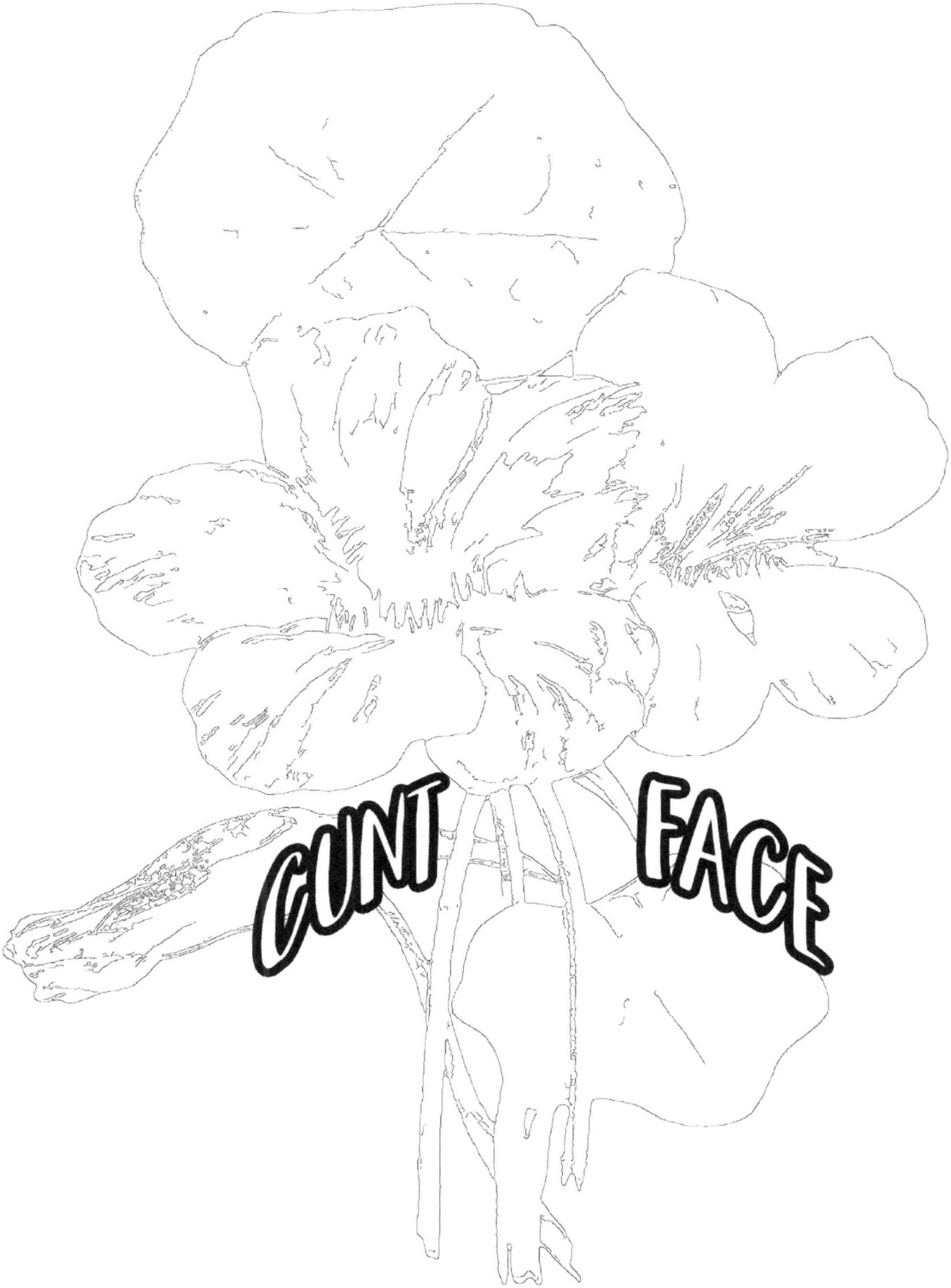
CUNT FACE

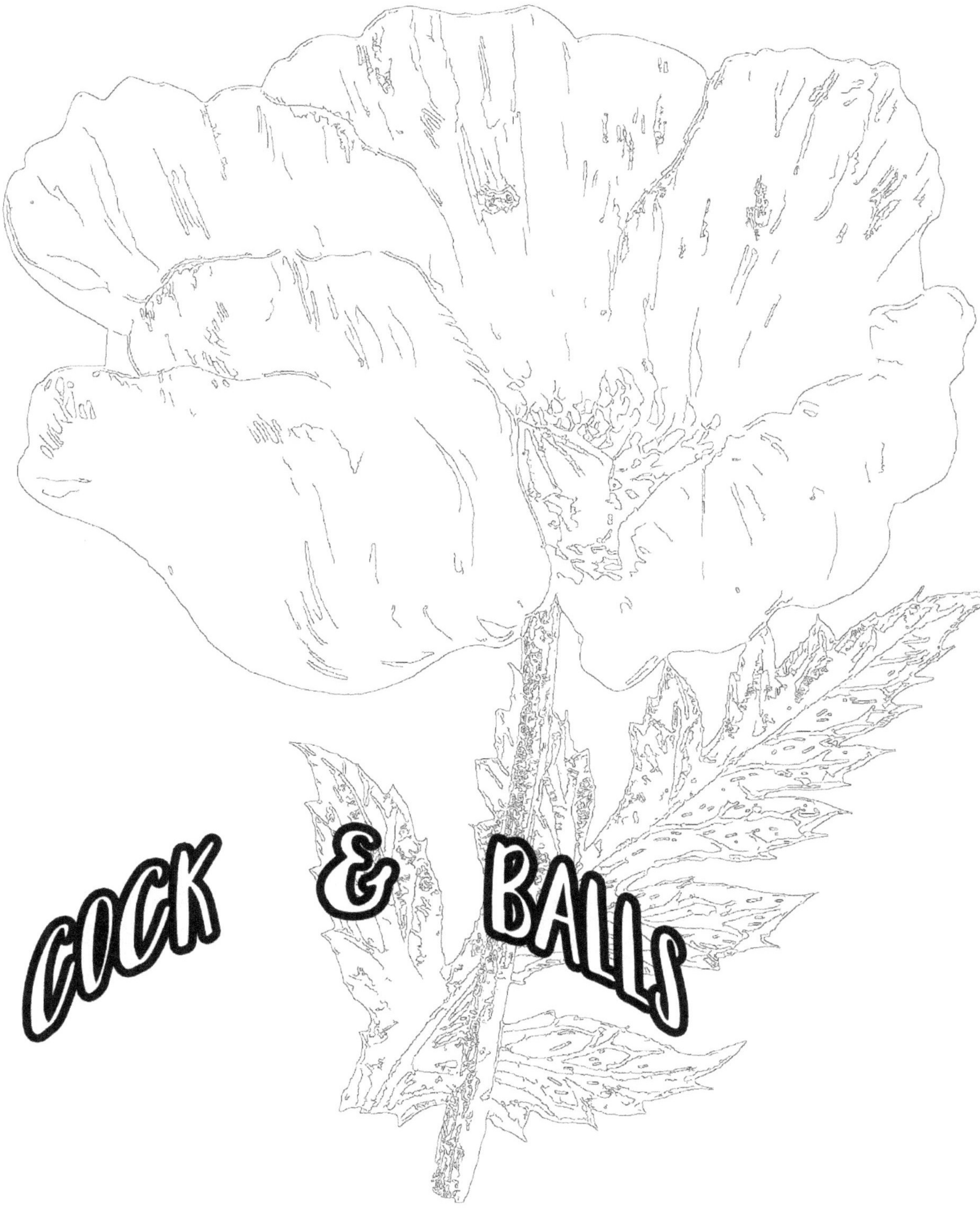
COCK & BALLS

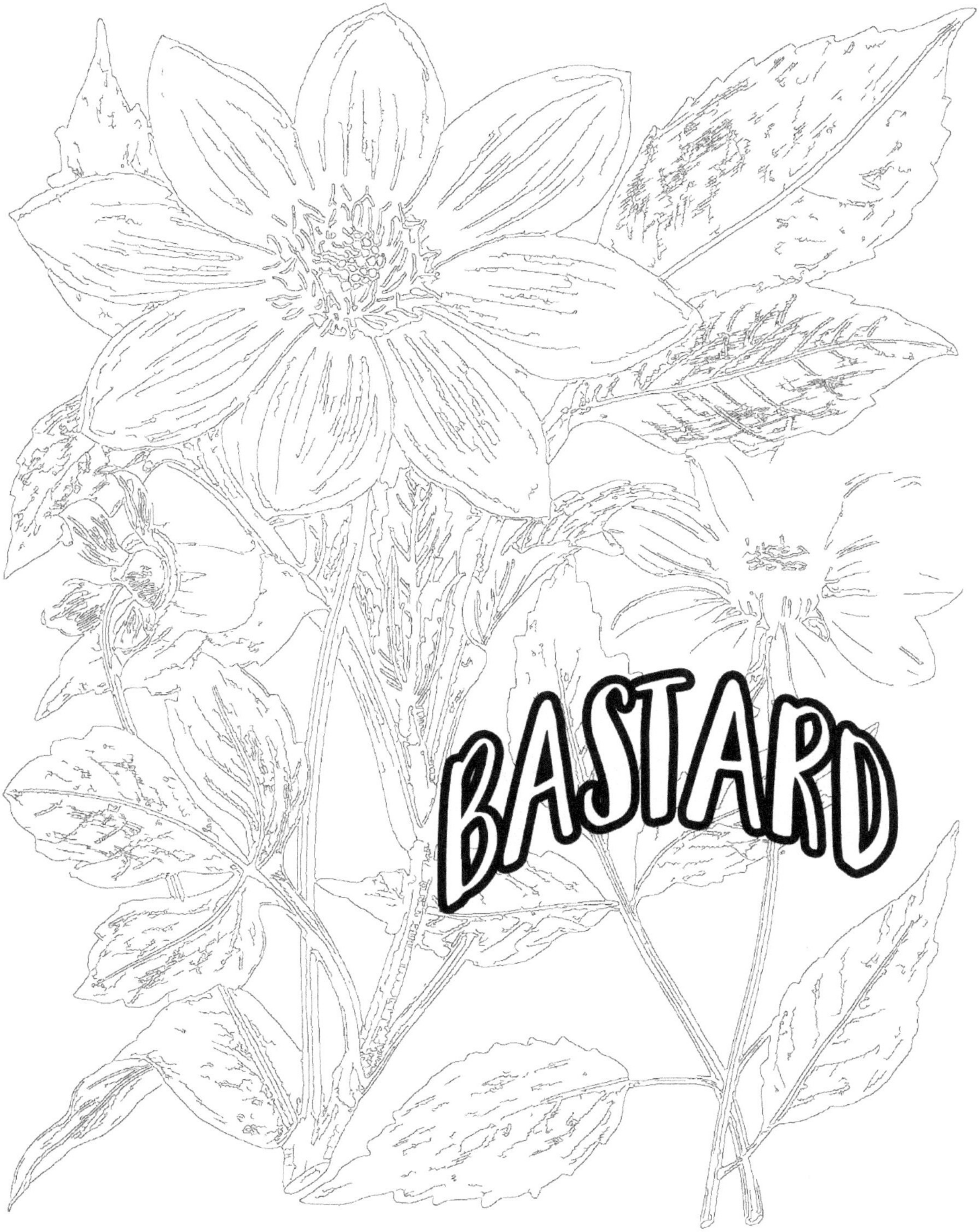
BASTARD

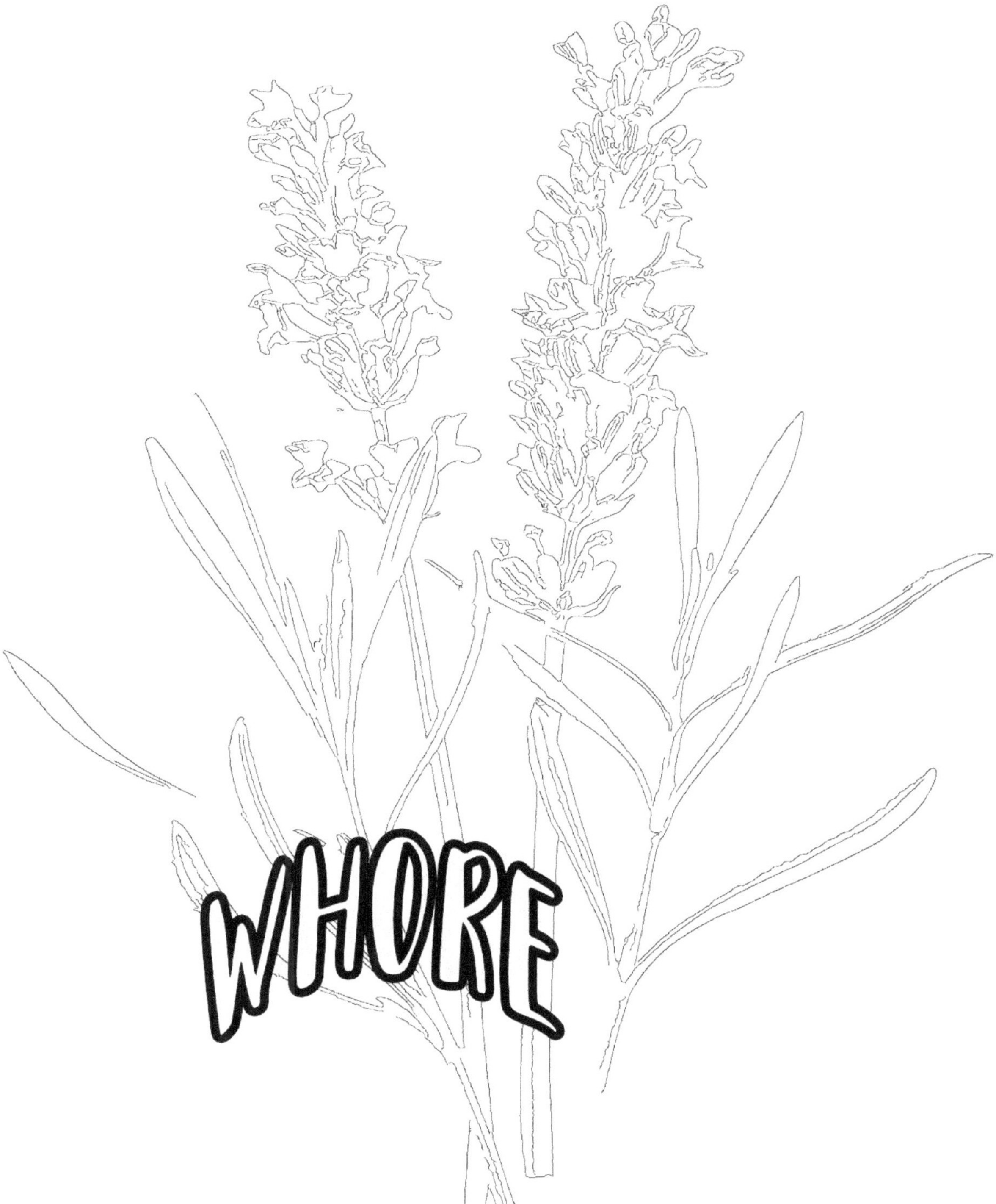
WHORE

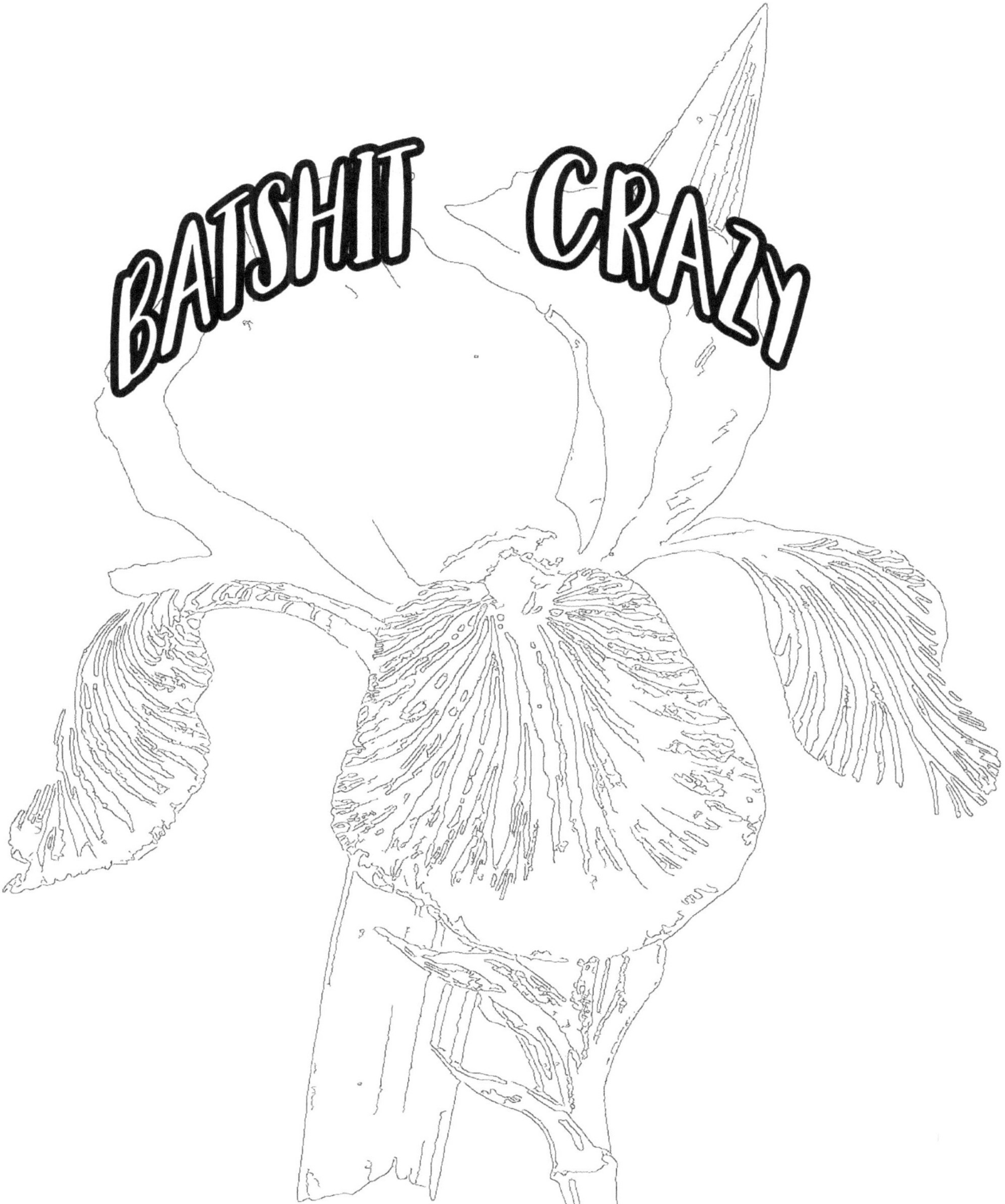
BATSHIT CRAZY

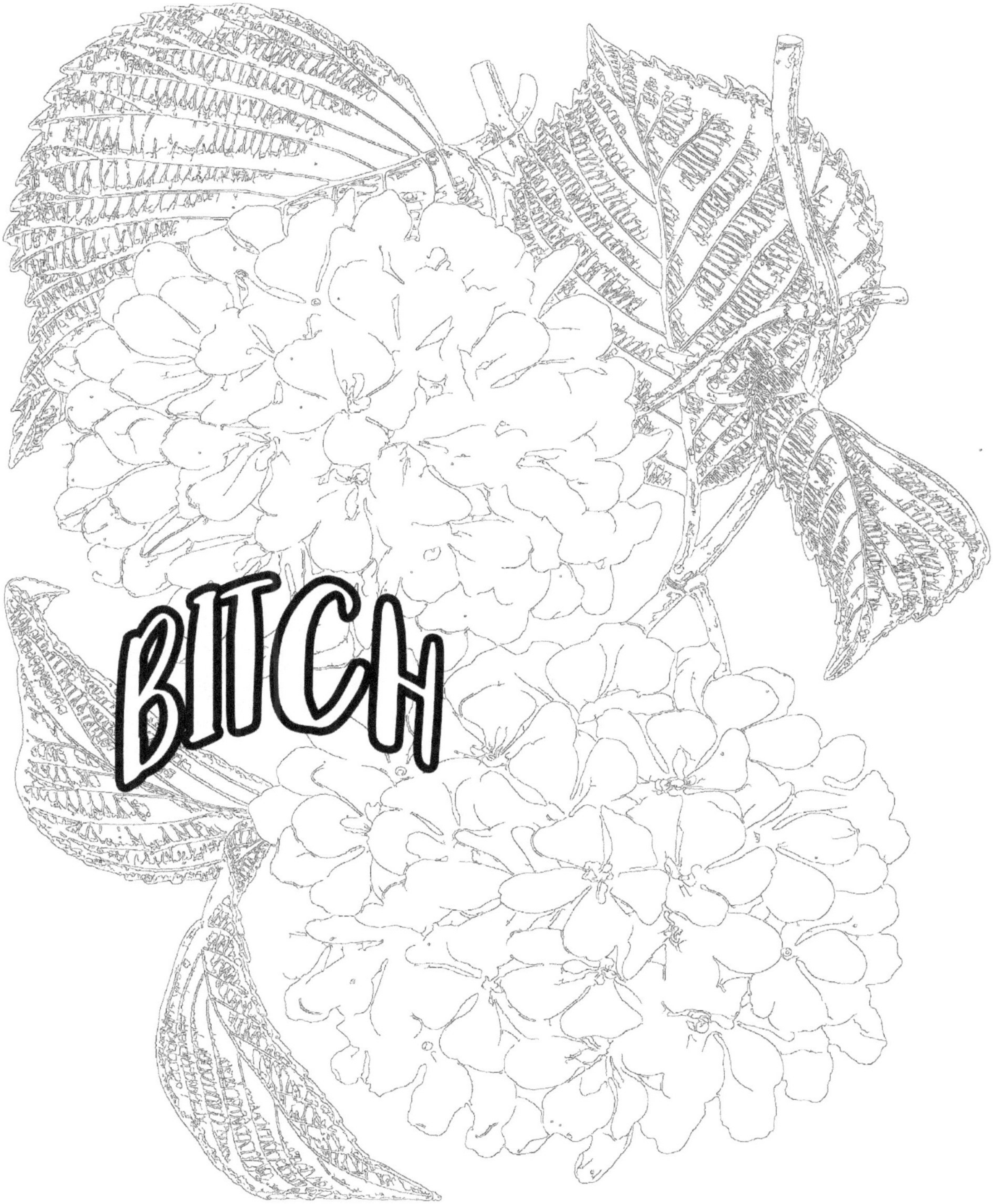
BITCH

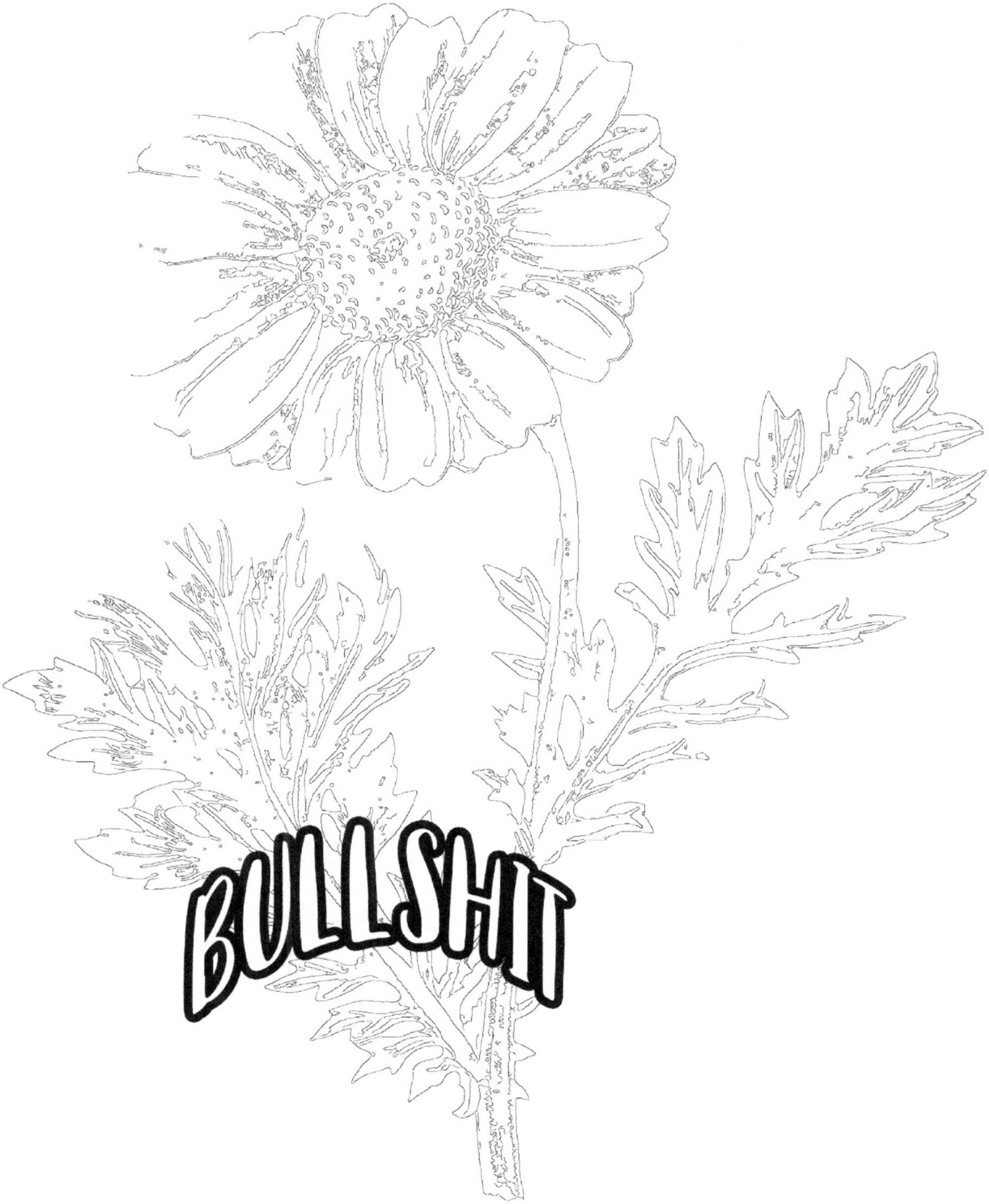
BULLSHIT

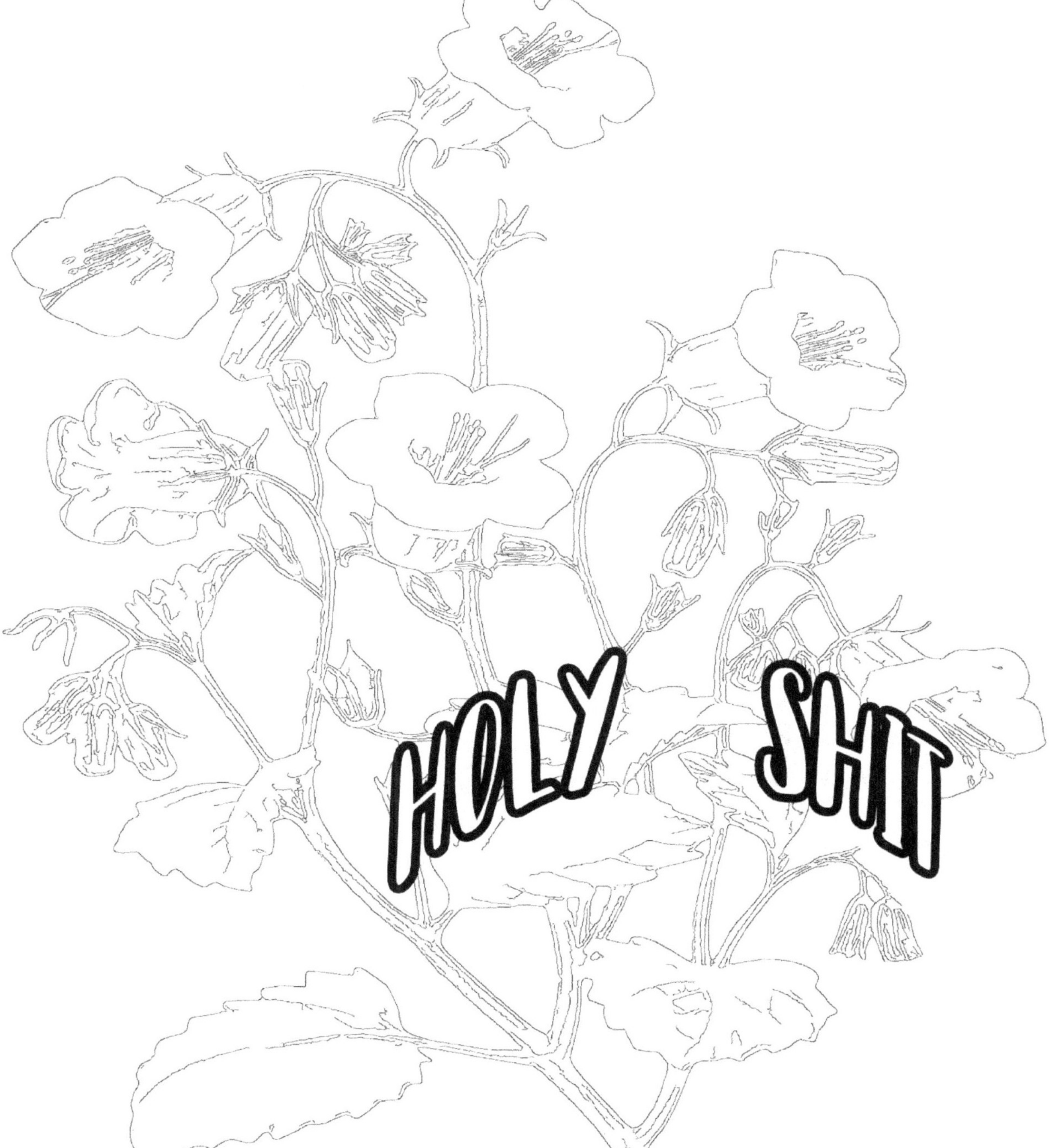
HOLY SHIT

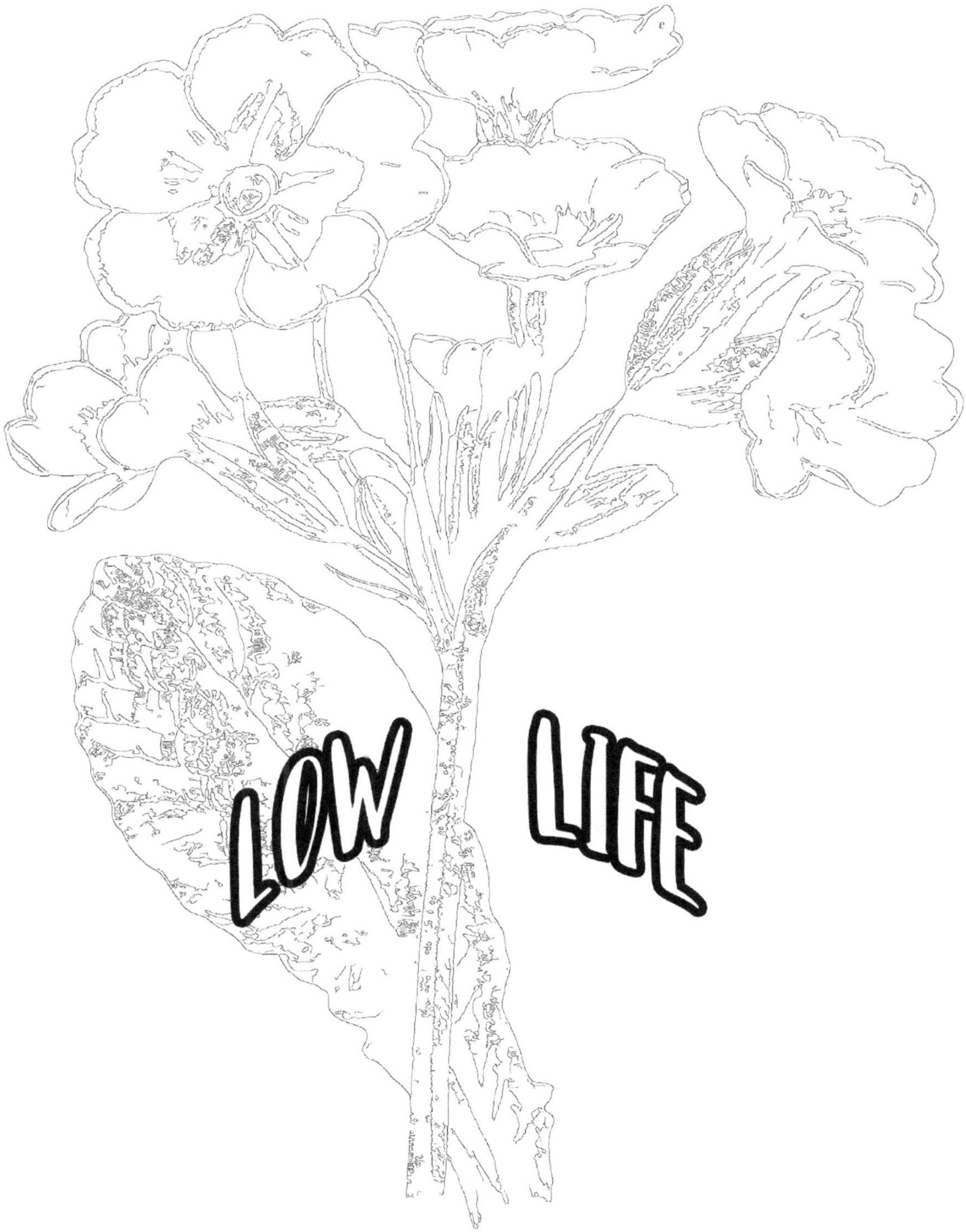
LOW LIFE

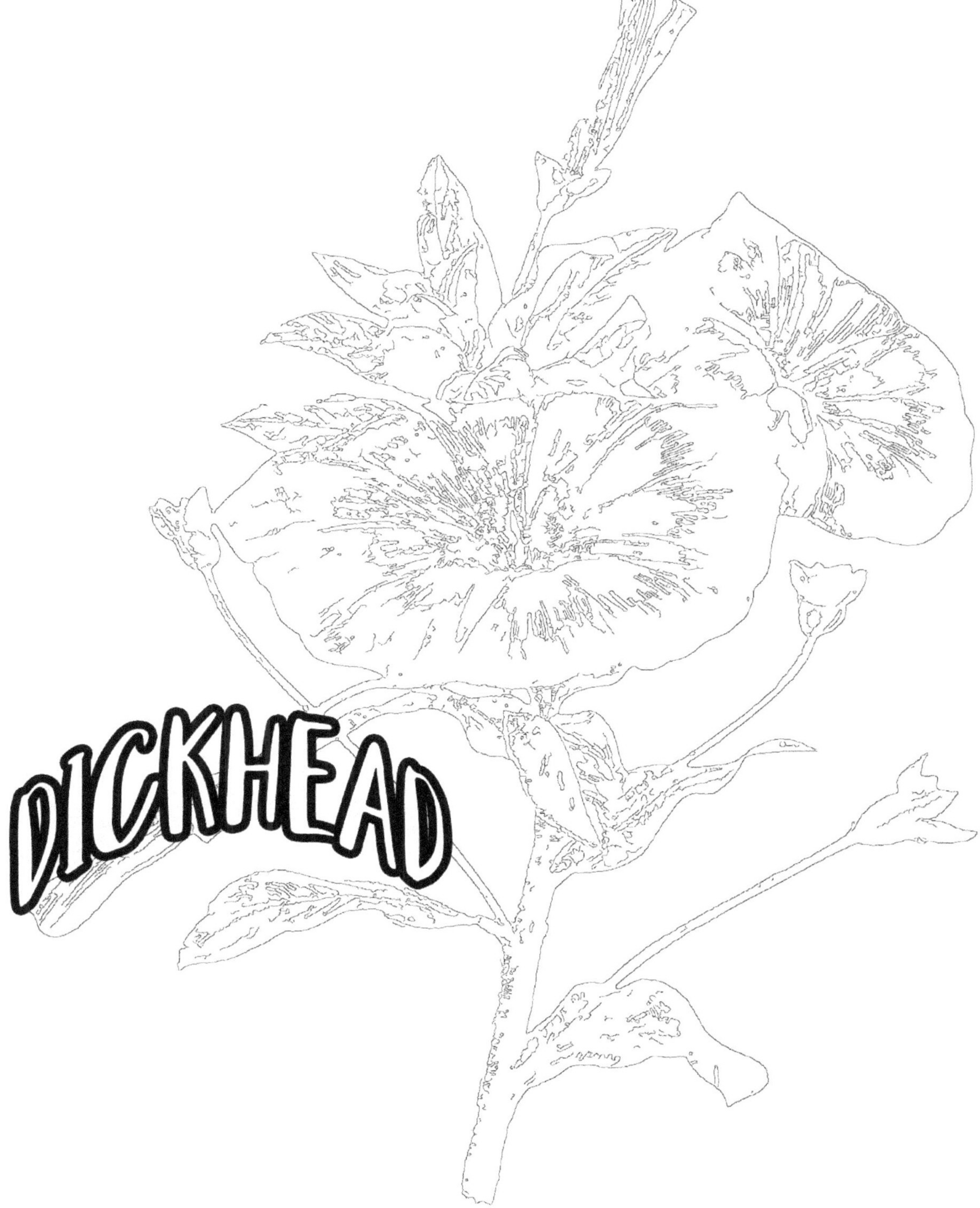
DICKHEAD

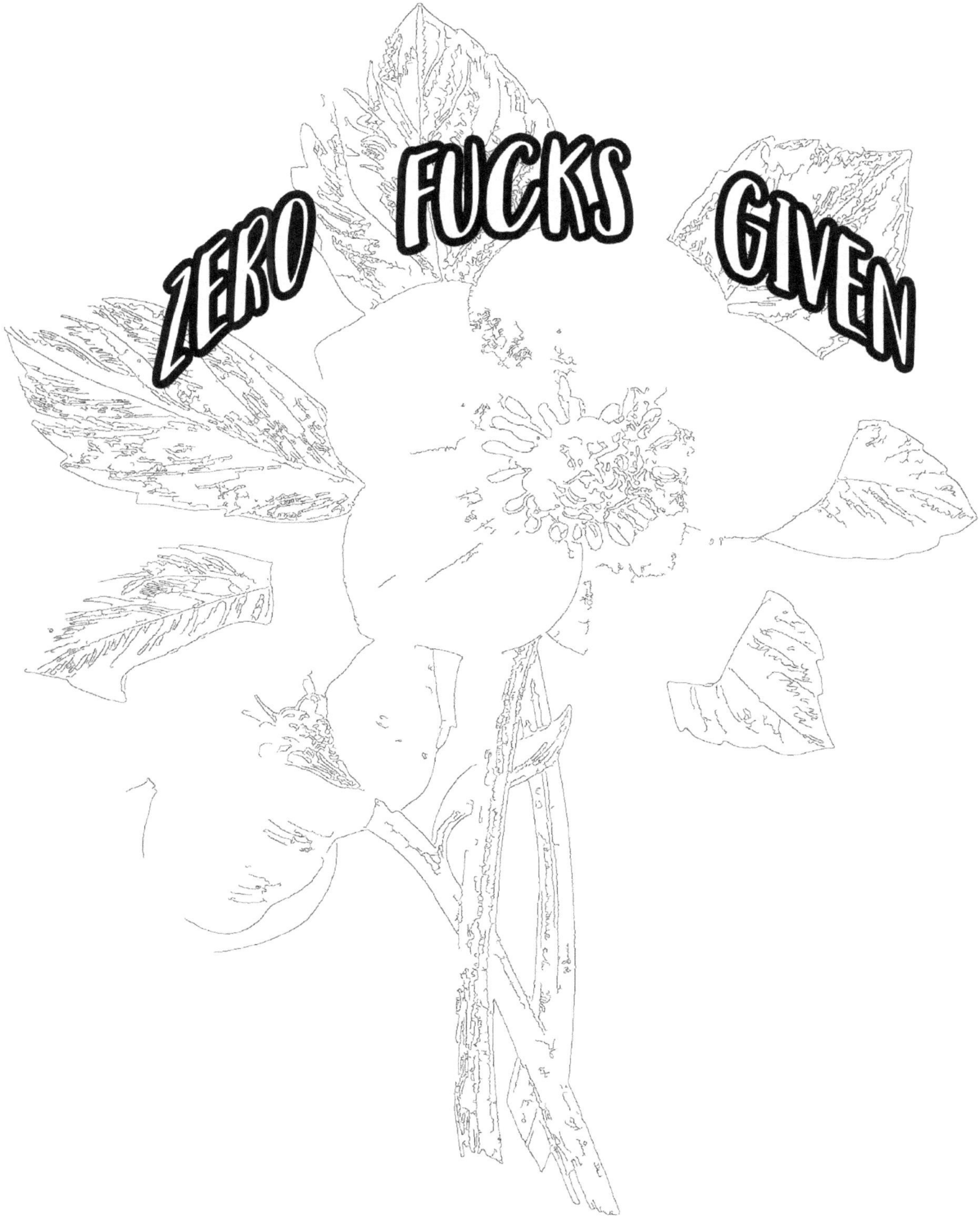
ZERO FUCKS GIVEN

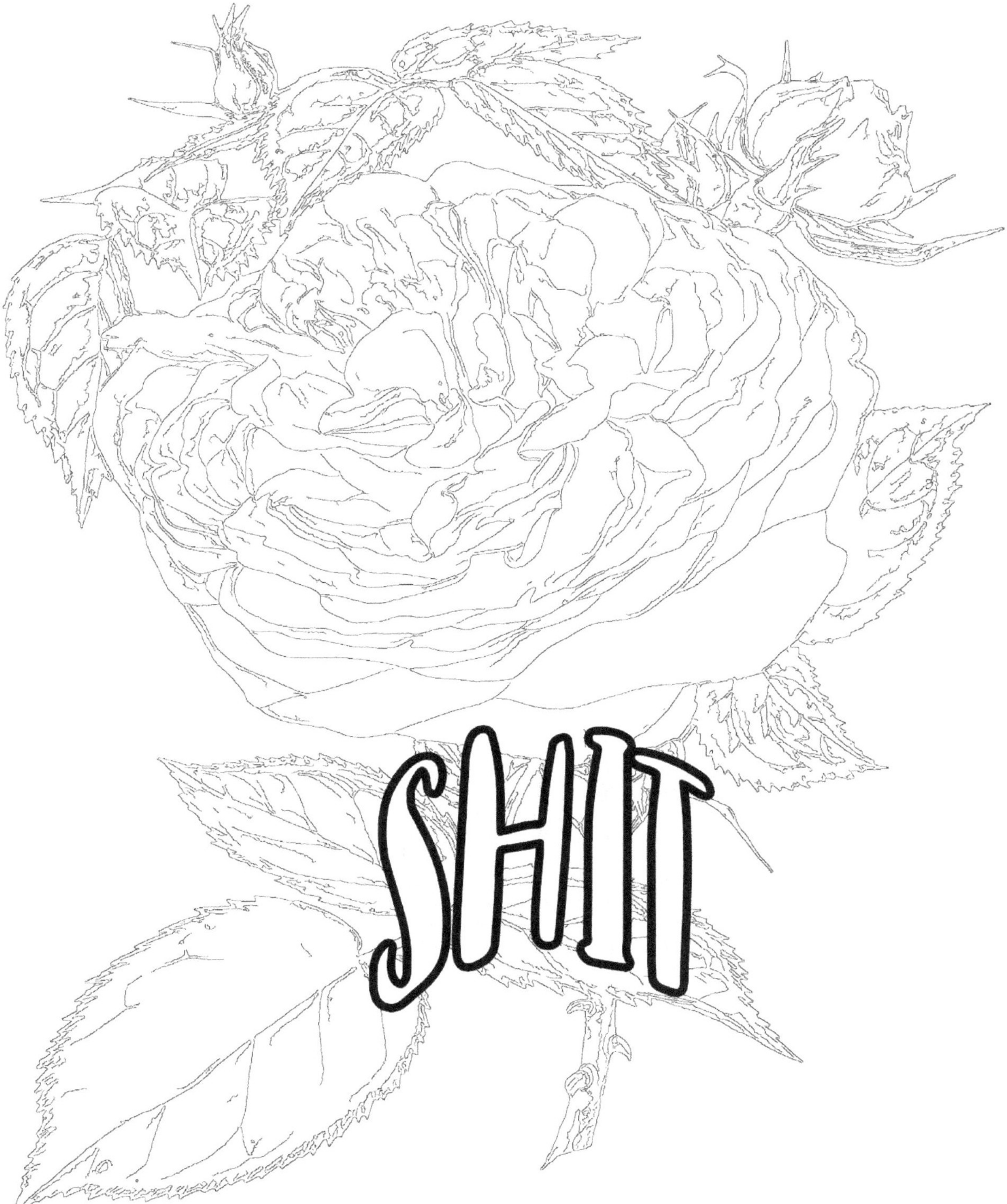
SHIT

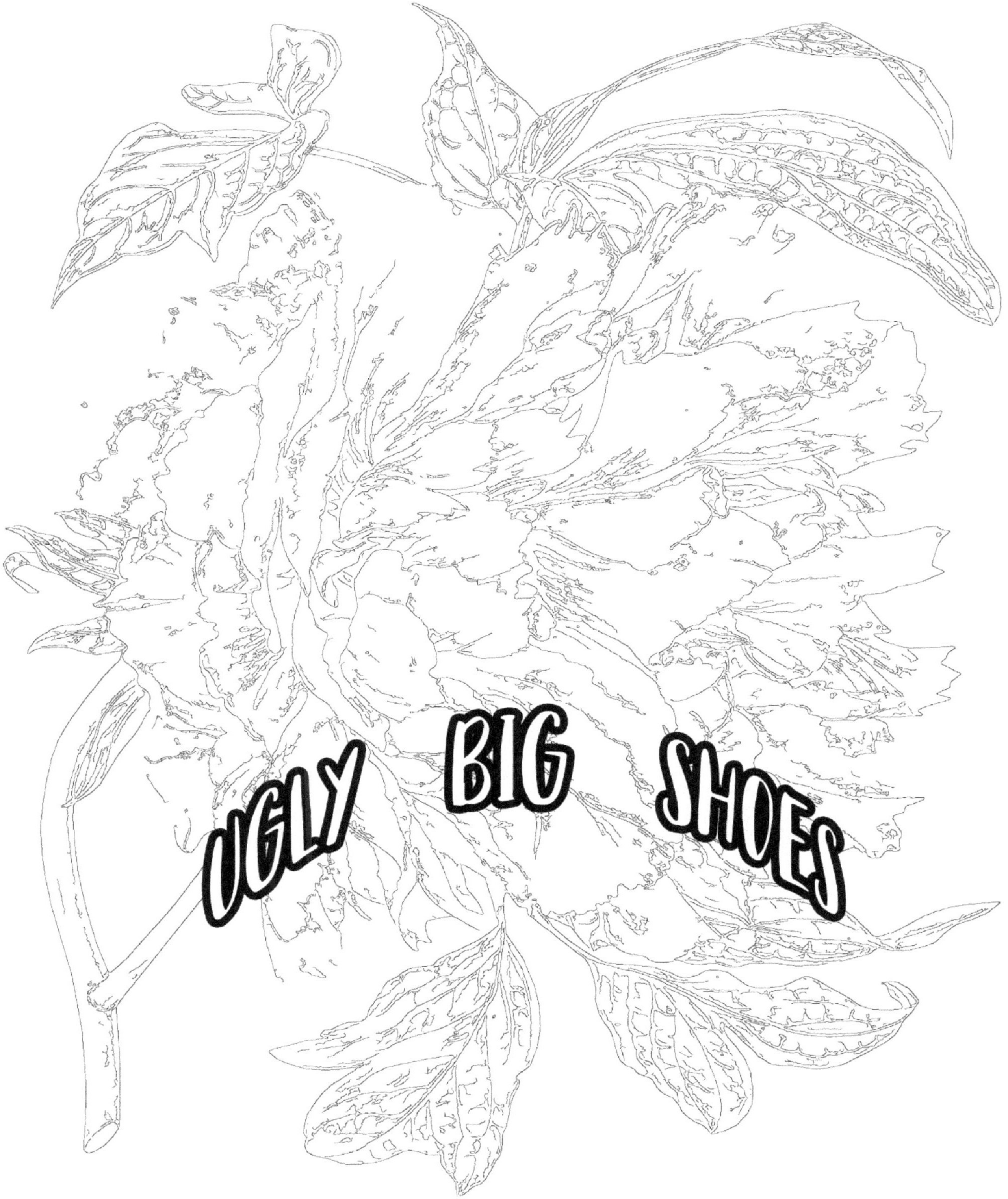
UGLY BIG SHOES

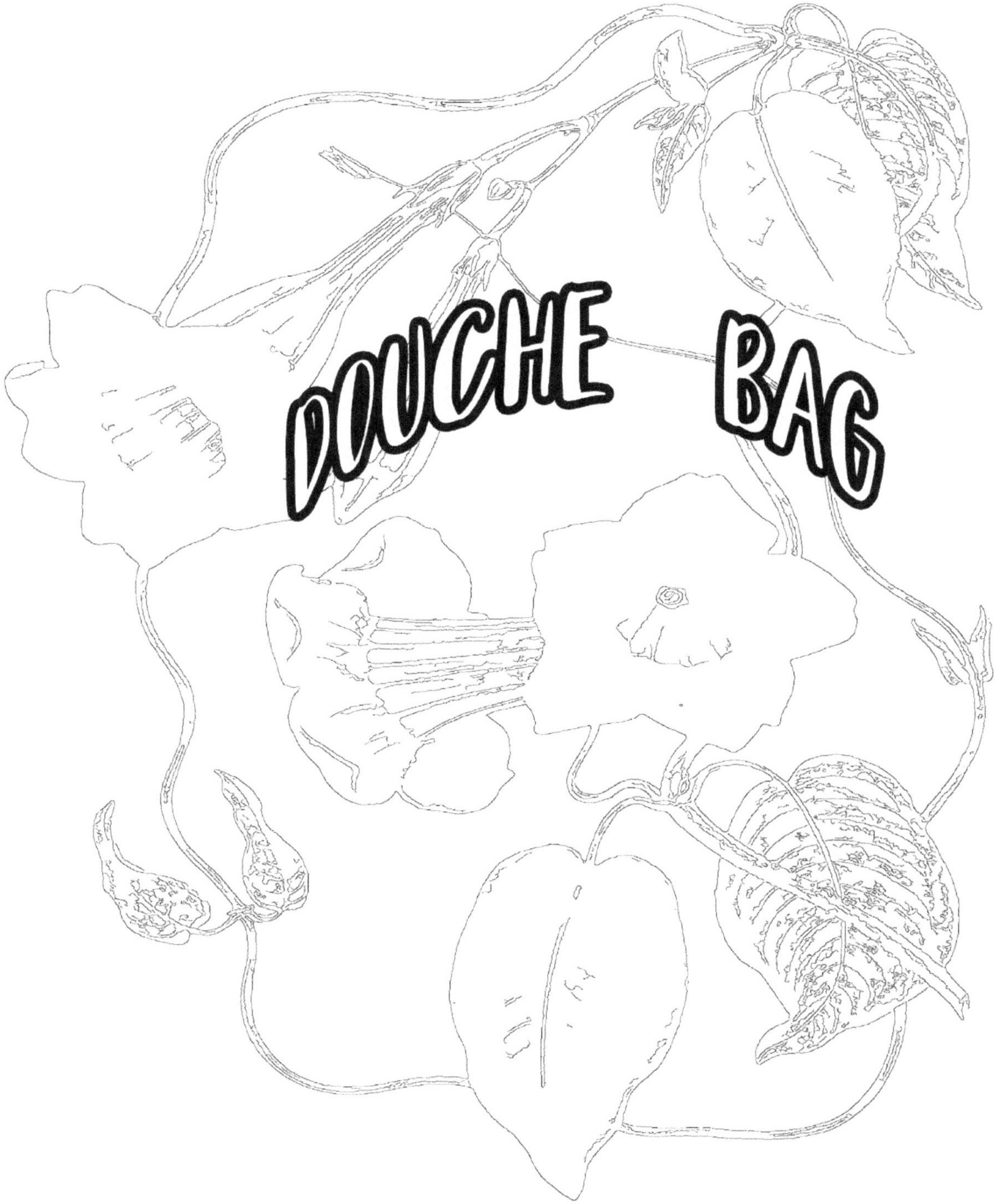
DOUCHE BAG

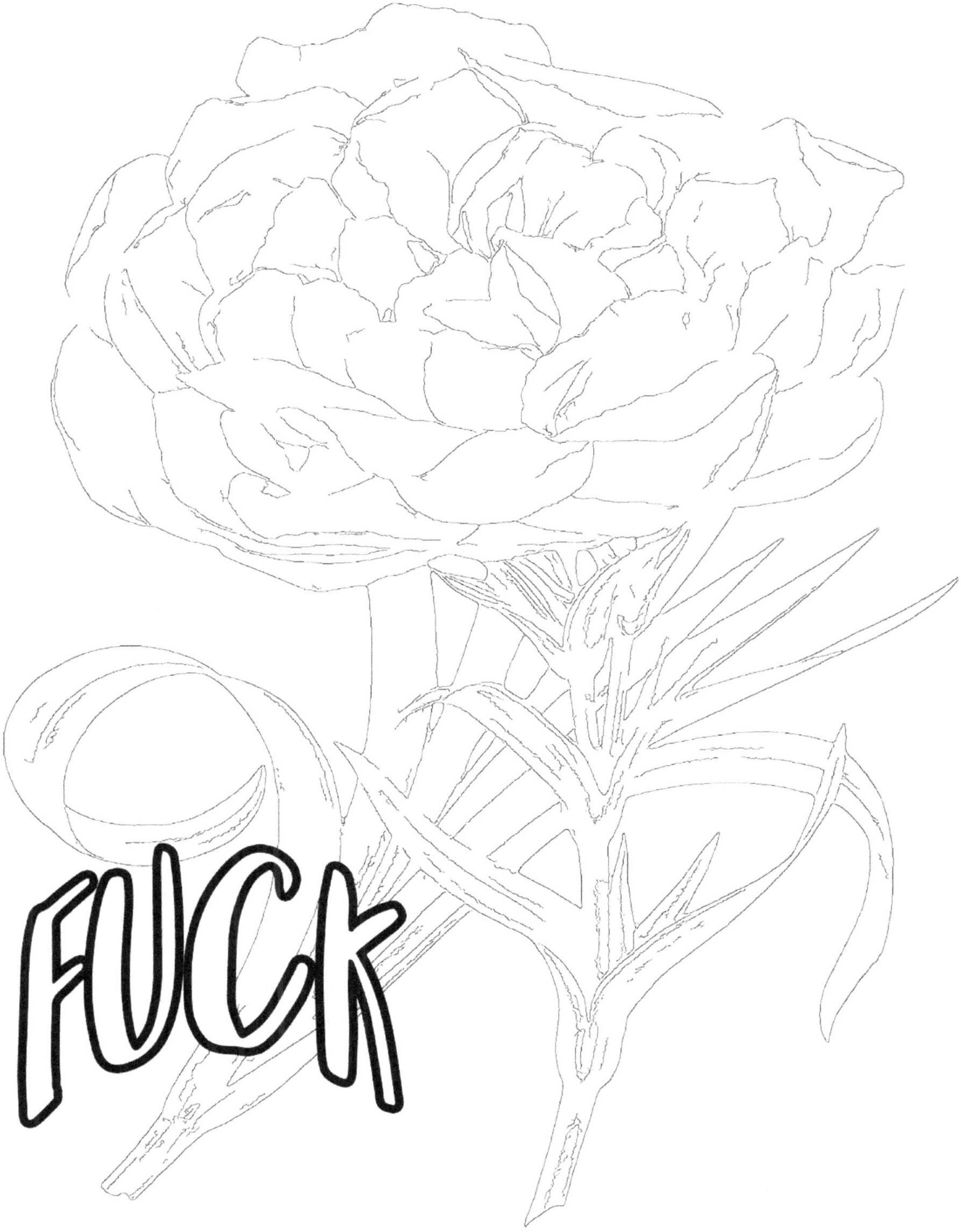
FUCK

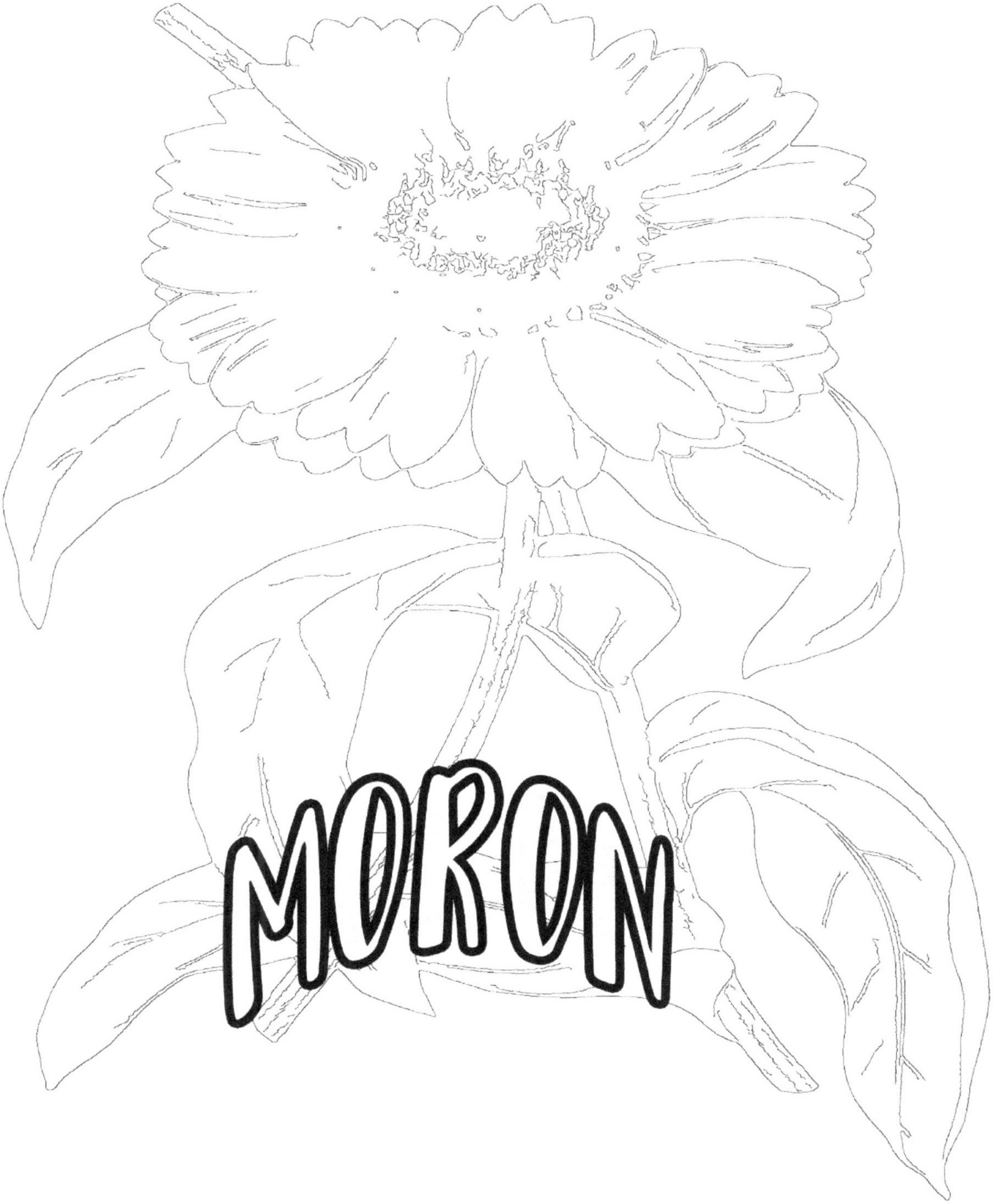
MORON

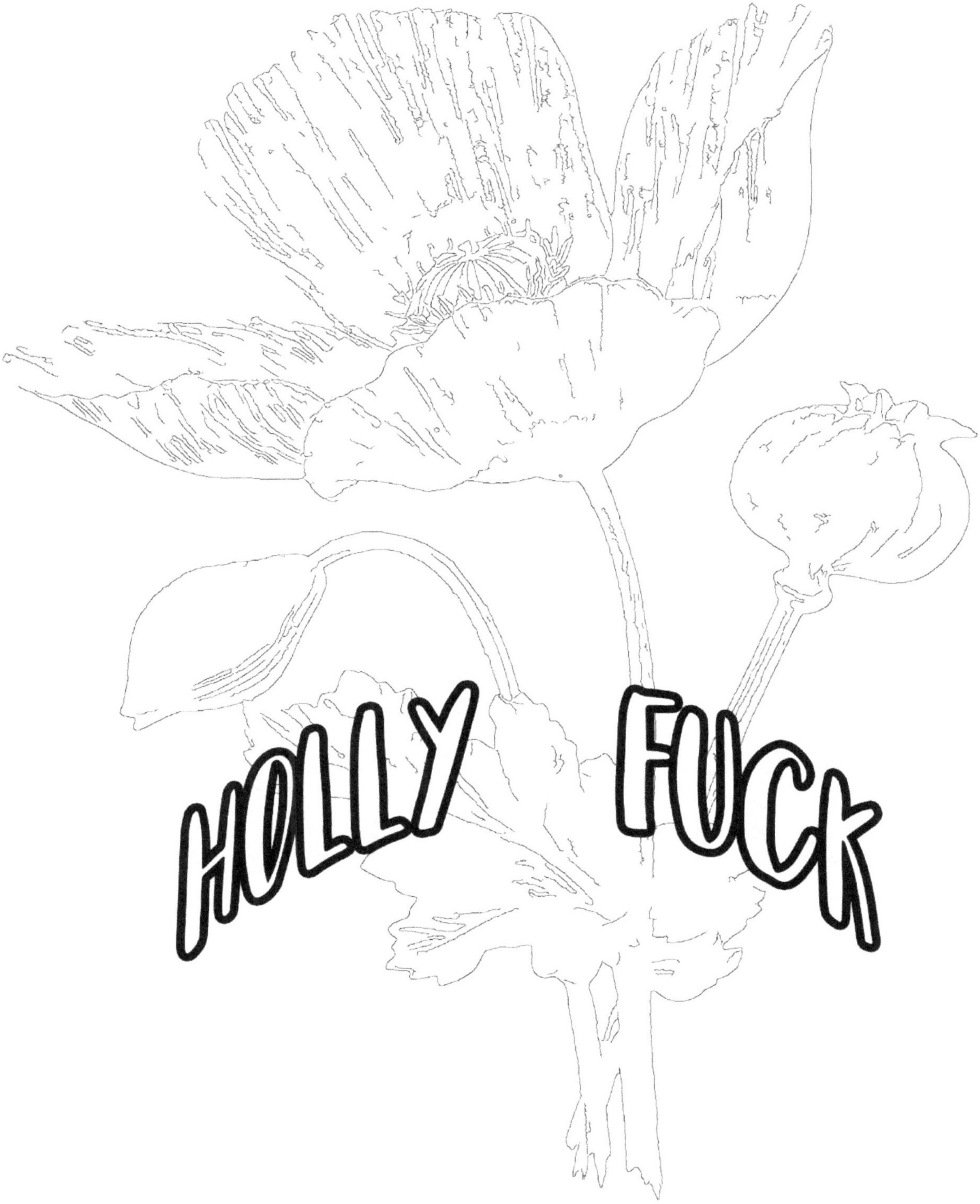
HOLLY FUCK

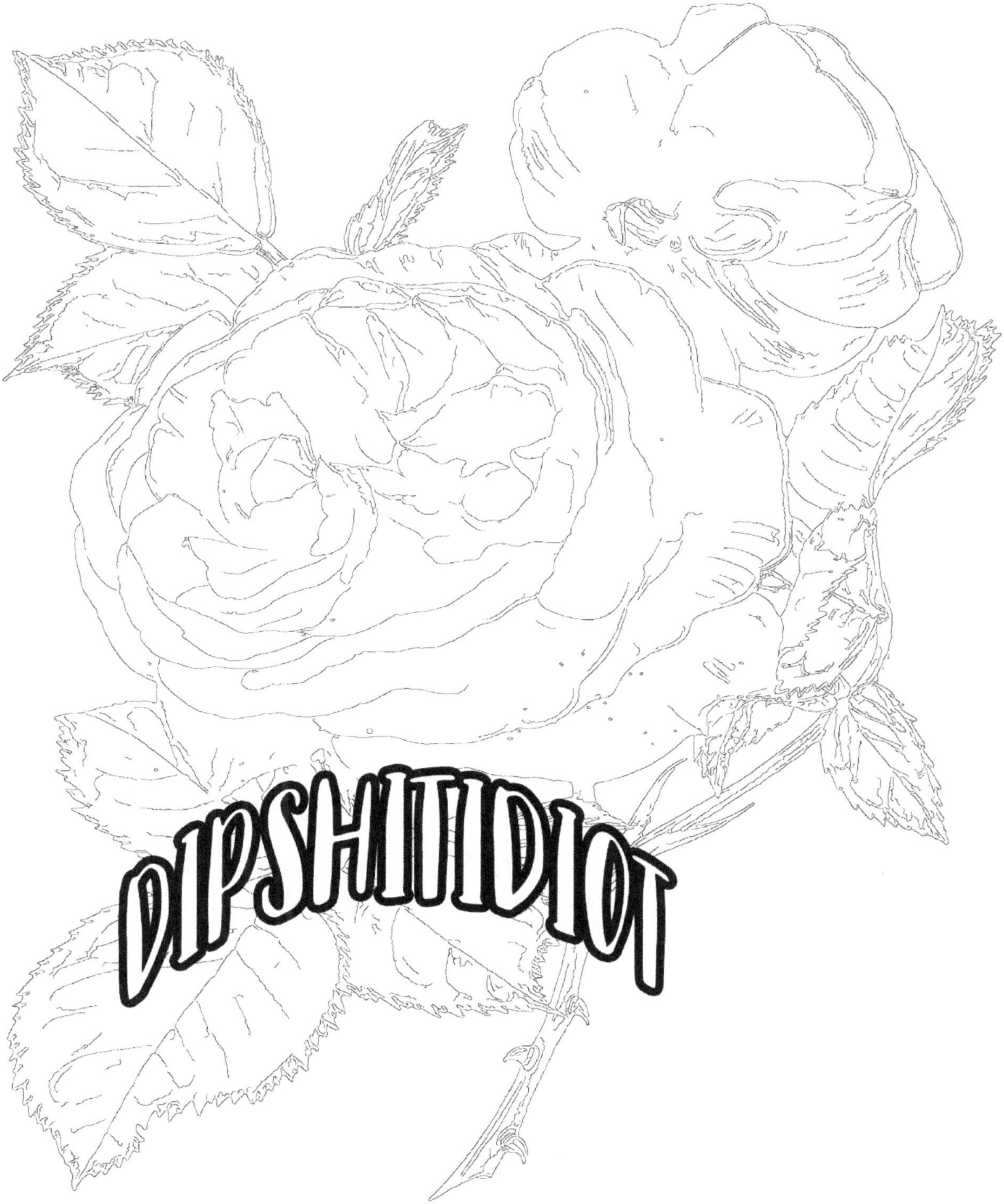
DIPSHITIDIOT

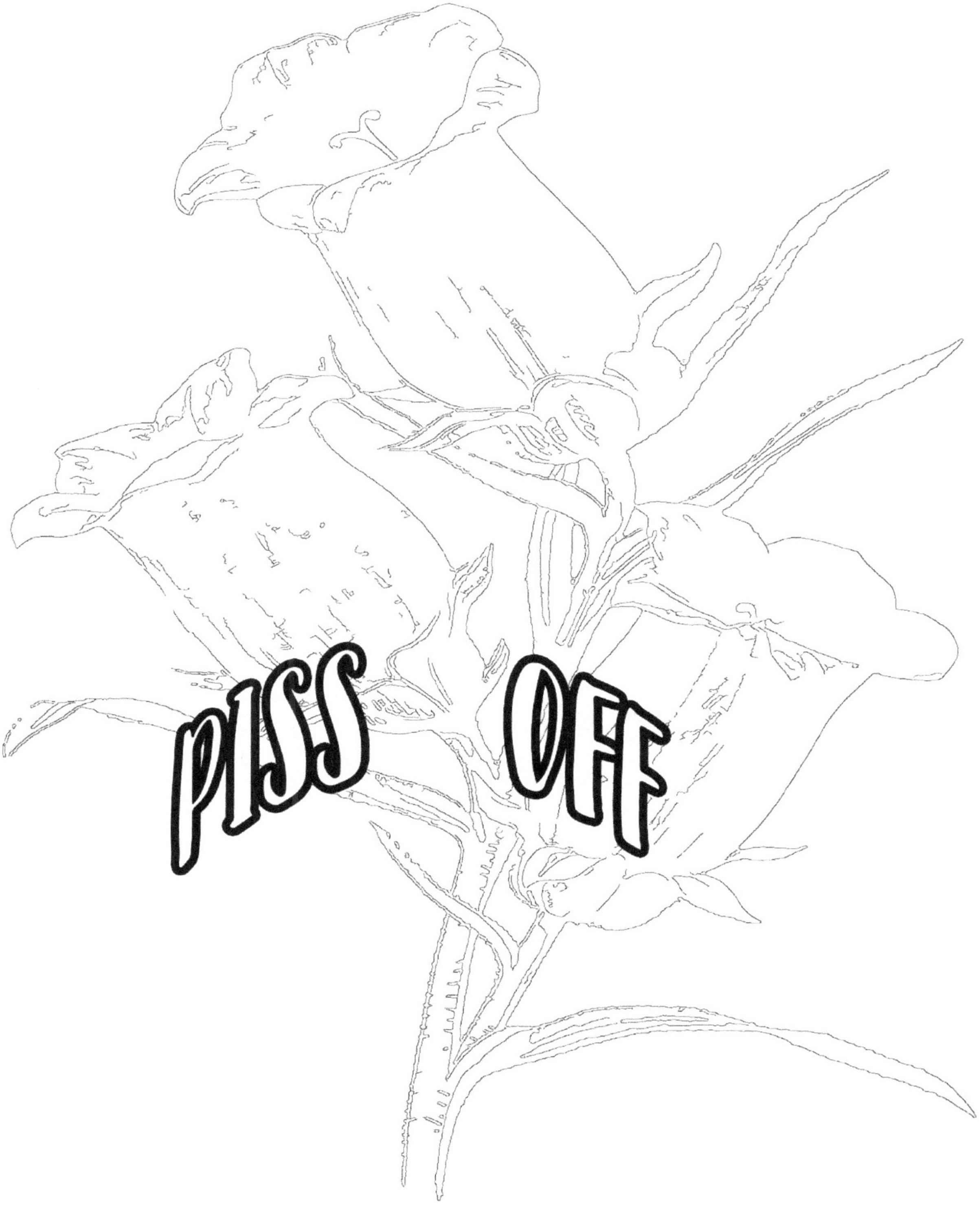
PISS OFF

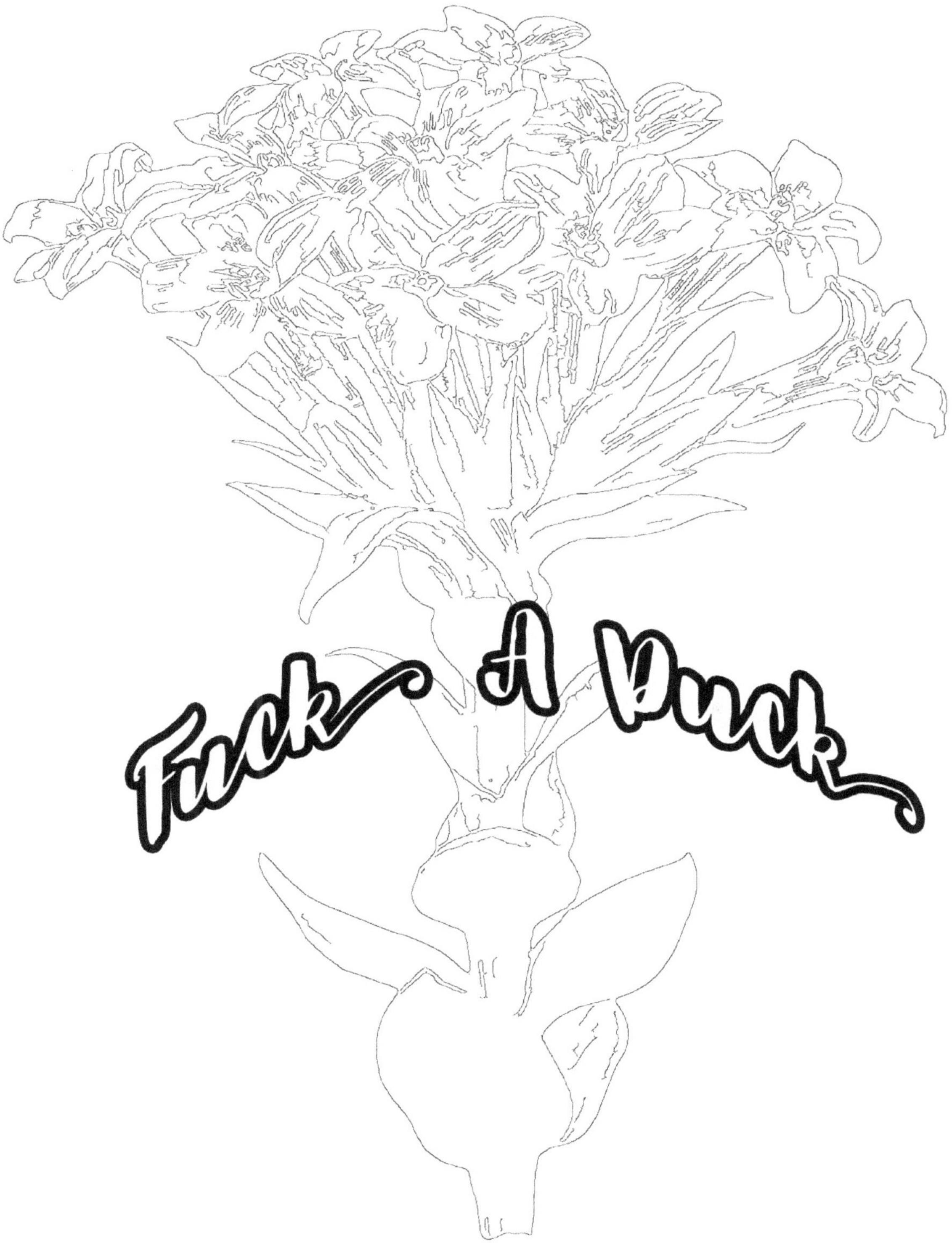
Fuck A Duck

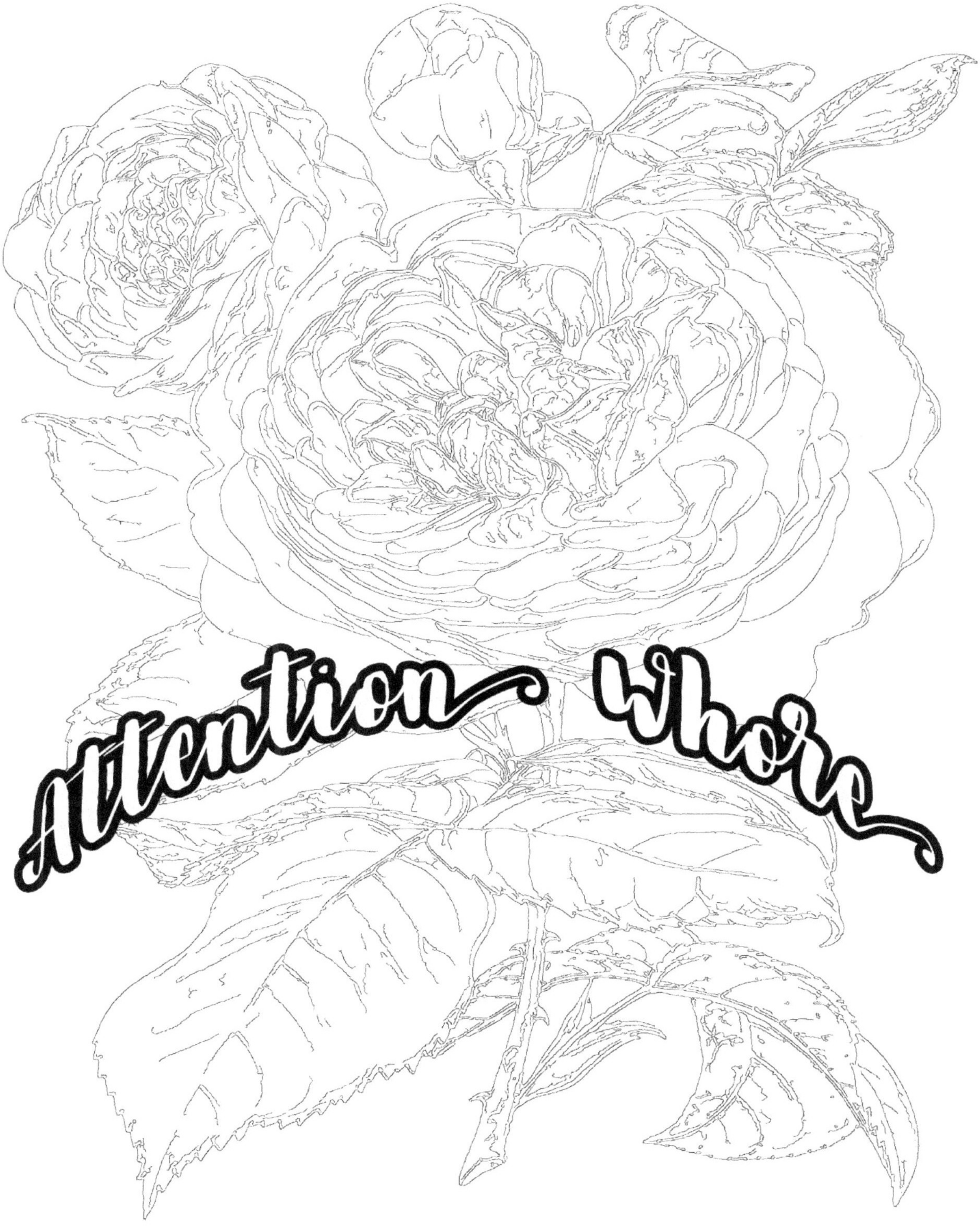
Attention Whore

www.ingramcontent.com/pod-product-compliance
Lightning Source LLC
Chambersburg PA
CBHW081620220526
45468CB00010B/2963